A typical fair day on the village green

Den
My
Uncle
So a stranger rears your child:

A Duo Biography
By
Oliver Keane

First published in 2009 by
Revilo production publications
Bishopstown, Cork City, Ireland.
www.oliverkane.com

Text © 2009 O.K.

Editing Design and Layout 2009-reviloproductions

All rights reserved. No part of this book may be utilised or reproduced in any form or by any means mechanical or electronic, including, photocopying, filming, recording, video recording, or by any information storage and retrieval system. nor shall by way of trade or otherwise be lent, resold or otherwise circulated in any form, of binding or cover other than that in which it is published without prior permission in writing from the publisher.

Den My Uncle. Copyright © Revilo Production Publications
® Revilo Productions Publications.™:

Dedication

Dedicated to the man I called Uncle Den.
Celebrating the goodness and kindness of humanity
By
Oliver Keane

Life is Complicated

I really have ten uncles
Once I thought I had none
And the man that became my father
I called him Uncle you see
When I found all my uncles,
so much time had passed in between,
they all seem like strangers to me.
Because the Uncle I knew he was real.
All the other uncles I found out that I had.
All dead and gone when I found them
All except one.
A very old man.
A saintly one.

Acknowledgements

To all people surrounding this story

Were present

Now where we dont know

We once met

We never knew

Copyright © 2009-A Revilo Production Publication

OLIVER KEANE

Den
My
Uncle

Copyright © 2009-A Revilo Production Publication

He was an old farmer who worked his farm seven days a week in the heartland of West Cork, he would rise every morning, during winter time at daybreak; and during summer rising time was with the dawn chorus.
Now he is ready to share his knowledge and years of hard work with this new little boy who has come into his life.
Its not easy being a father to a child.
Especially a child, who is not your own.'
but things have a way of creeping up on one-self.
He could see in the eyes of the child a fear,
and knowing his own limits, it became a road to his final years on this earth.
Having never gone to school himself,
from the outset no one would suspect that he could neither read or write:
He had the exceptional ability to work his farm,
care for his animals and put aside time for church and card playing, as his few short years were fast disappearing.
In a special way he made every effort to impart his knowledge to this child, a stranger who has now become more of a companion than a child.
Uncle was a tall man who always wore a hat, he had three hats.!
One for Sunday wear, one for going to places such as to the fair or the creamery, and the hat he used when he would be toiling in the fields.
His face always in need of a shave, a thing he would do

every Saturday night before going to confession.
He would fetch the leather strap apply some oil allowing it to soak into the leather,
meanwhile he would fill a bowl of tobacco and smoke his pipe:'
Then he would run his cut-throat razor up and down the leather strap constantly checking
to see if the edge was sharp enough to shave the tough silver week long stubble from off his face.
Uncle I said to him am I a lucky boy, !
yeah he replied you are a very lucky boy, do you remember when you first came here, I do I replied.
Well he said did you know how to milk a cow or sharpen a scythe when you came here, no I said I did not, and you have so much more to learn he would always say to me:
often I would say Uncle what is the moon made of, he would look at me and smile through his wrinkly weather beaten face, his reply was always the same, I only answer to things I know about.
Well then Uncle tell me what is the earth made of, ah now we are getting somewhere, the earth is full of clay and rock and water.
full of living things that live off the clay the rock and the water'
Uncle would get the white blue rimmed enamel dish, go to the barrel where the drainpipe filled it from the constant showers, bring it in about half full, then take the huge black kettle from off the swinging gantry

and pour in the boiling water until it was the exact
temperature he desired for his shave.
The shaving was a weekly ritual, I would watch him as he
rolled up his sleeves up above his elbows,
his huge calloused hands,
swollen and blistered from hard farm work,
he would then fold down the rim of his shirt, as the shirt
did not have a collar,
Shirt collars were a separate item of clothing usually
attached to the shirt with brass or bone studs.
All the while the red bar of lifebuoy soap is softening in
dish of warm water'
After applying the soap all over his beard, he would rub
it viciously until he got a thick lather,
Then he would draw the cut-throat in gently strokes
downward across his cheeks,
revealing his vinous skin.
At each stroke of the razor a big lump of soapy lather
containing the shaven hair would be diligently wiped off
the blade with his forefinger and placed in an old broken
cup.
Immersing his face into the dish and throwing back his
head into the towel,
ah we're right now for another week.'
Its Saturday evening, the cows have been milked, all are
in their stalls,
the days hard work has been done, so all that remains
now is to tackle up the pony and trap, then put on the
Sunday best and trot off to the village for confession.

The soul has to be kept pure and free from sin, as no one knows the hour of our calling.
Devotions will be on at the church, followed by benediction,
all of course in Latin,
Uncle same as all the rest:' will not have clue what is being said, everything the priest would say would be taken for granted." verbatim "
All the women and children at one side of the church and all the men at the other side,
the social behaviour akin to the sinking titanic,
women and children first followed by the older men followed by the younger men.
After confession it was straight home in the dark,
the only light apart from the moon and stars would be the brass polished carbide lamp that shone out from the right hand shaft of the pony trap.
The smell of the well oiled harness permeated the night air with its linseed oil to ward off the effects of harsh weather which makes the harness very rigid hard and brittle.
Every now and then while the pony is trotting, she would sort of skip a step,
some times I would be thinking that the pony might trip and fall as I do when I run too fast;'
but it never happens our pony.
Sparks shoot out through the darkness as the pony's well shod hoofs make contact with larger stones among the pebbles gravel and grey clay that makes up the boreen

surface leading from the main road to our house.
Sunday morning comes, no breakfast, not a bite would be eaten.
Only fresh spring water from the blue and white enamel bucket, with its aerated lid to keep out the flies and allow air to circulate.
The soul of the man would be kept as pure as possible ready to receive holy communion body and blood of our Lord Jesus Christ.
Uncle would remain very tight lipped between confession and communion, in case any foul words may emanate from his mouth.
He would not listen to the radio because he may overhear something or other that may cause him to have unclean thoughts.
And he certainly would not go playing cards, messing with the devils prayer book he would say.
The pony and trap scenario of last night would be repeated minus the carbide lamp.
Green straw/horsehair sprung leather seats surrounds the inside of the pony trap.
These seats are looking splendid against the brown varnished woodwork, an embellished brass rail with its two lovely circles on either side allowing the reins would run through;
Complimented by the black iron forged step at the back leading to the trap door.
Uncle I would ask him, will I have a pony and trap when I get big.

Of course you will he would say, maybe you might have two of them, no one knows. He would tell me that when he was a small boy they did not have a pony trap, just an ordinary horse and cart.
I loved the pony/trap I would sit in it for hours when it was parked up in the cart house,
with its long slender shafts tied up towards to roof.,
I would imagine myself trotting along a road of no return, just going on and on for ever.
Now that mass is over and we are all very hungry, its dinner time and the bacon cabbage and spuds are nearly ready, hurryingly its consumed, and its off a hunting for the evening or a least until milking time.
We would all be very hungry after our afternoon hunting we usually begin the hunt by observing the fields,
looking for small pathways worn by the traffic of wild animals, our two black hounds are nervous and ready for the off:'
It's the terriers who do the rooting, going down into the burrows, to chase out fox's.
A fox is a very clever animal. So clever are they, that they have two entrances to their den,
Sometimes it's a vain hunt when we try to capture Reynard as he is known, we could spend the entire afternoon chasing him, only to find out that we have been on a wild goose chase.
A fox can send out a call to other fox's, who in turn will

take up the flight.
Two or three fox's can tire out an entire set of hunting dogs, the dogs think they are after the same fox, and in the process they get ran into the ground.!
Not much luck today Uncle would say, as we packed up our expedition for today, but sure there's always next Sunday, and the Sunday after that.
My job of work each day before I go to school is to milk the kerry cow.
A tough animal to get milk from, I have to sing to her, so that she relaxes enough to let the milk flow.
One of the nice things about her is, she comes when I call her, on my way home from school I see her in a field, kera kera, I shout, and up to the fence she runs to me.
I have been told to be careful with her.
Cattle can swing their heads side to side, if one is standing too near can be hit by their horns, a very painful experience.
But for now my favourite is, actually I have two favourites, my most favourite is Bell my dog, given to me two days after I arrived here.
My next favourite is Betsy my goat, she like me is growing up.
Uncle says she is passing me out.
Because next year she will be a mammy as he puts it, so she will be having babies I ask him, yes he says.
Kid goats, you will love them.
Also he says they are very tasty.

Then one day on my way home from school.
I see kera my friendly cow lying on the side of the road, three men standing over her, one of them, the veterinary surgeon.
When I draw near, I see her breathing her last breaths, I feel sick.
Uncle tells me not to worry.
The vet looks at me, smiling he says she is going to cow heaven, ah well that's not too bad.
Now she is being dragged to a hole that uncle along with another farmer had dug earlier that day, after the veterinary surgeon had called to check the herd of cows for the dreaded disease TB.!
She had failed the test, so they put her down and she was duly buried covered in quicklime at the end of a disused field in the farm.
Uncle I could see had tears in his eyes I could hear him muttering some prayers for her and for all his animals and every animal.
Sometimes I can hear him getting hot under the collar and really mad, for instance when he would discover that rats had infested one or two of the root vegetable pits.
He'd go about swearing at the cats telling them what a useless job they are doing.
Traps would be set and poison laid out for the rats, eventually he would get rid of them.!
The root pits were quite big, a mangol pit would hold

three acres of root, and likewise the turnip pit, then there is also the potato pit.'
Cabbage will be left in the ground and harvested as required, Uncles cows had a great variety of food, so they are very happy cows,.
He would groom them, trim their tails, always checking their hoofs, as cows can get hoof rot from standing in wet fields or anywhere with too much moisture underfoot.
Some cows are allowed to rear their own calf's, mother cow being very protective at first then a few months go by
And its as if they become strangers, each going their own separate way.
Uncle a proud man when it came to horses, they are always treated like royalty, only the best will do, he would rather go without himself than see the horses without.
He has three horses and a pony, two of the horses are especially for working the land,
the other horse is for the road, going to the creamery the fair day, and going for the shopping.
Whereas the pony was used for mass or going to an agricultural show, they being the only type of events that Uncle ever attends, perhaps an odd auction or two.
"No" Uncle never went very far away, always near his farm, the place he loved and cared for.
A few visits to Cork city in his lifetime three to be exact. often he would explode verbally arrah he'd say, sure tis

like a cackle of geese running away from a fox on a windy day. too much commotion.
City life is not for uncle.!
In the stillness of a misty foggy evening I would watch him as he would swing his sharp scythe cutting down about two cartloads of furze in the process.
As I would get near I could see droplets of moisture dripping off the silver unshaven beard, shaded by his brown greasy sweaty hat. now a sort of shiny grey, and when he moved his head the light would reflect off it; colours could be seen and in my thoughts I could see a rainbow.
Every now and then Uncle would take a quick short rest, a time to fill the pipe and take a short stroll to the stony fence surrounding the brake,
smoking in a brake of crispy dry volatile furze can be dangerous, one spark as she is off;
no stopping it, it would be over in a few minutes burned as black as coal.
On other occasions when Uncle would take a break' he shows me how to make a whistle from a small branch of a sycamore, its great fun sitting in then spring sunshine trimming a piece of soft fleshy sycamore. take a four inch length, with the handle of the penknife gently tap the bark all around, until it slides off tube like:'
Then cut a trap hole, as its called, then trim the mouthpiece area at an angle, finally cut I very shallow track along the top

rim, now wet the removed tube-bark, and slide over the carved inner, blow, blow. Yes it works, but the dogs are not agreeing:' certainly.!

The entire hillside is now shrouded in a thick fog, vision reduced to a few yards either side, the silence being broken only by the swishing of the scythe as it cuts through the hardy stemmed furze branches. a scattered swarth that lays behind resembling dead soldiers in some ancient battleground.

Every now and then the horse would get tired of standing still, rhythmically moving a step left and right, perhaps a backwards forwards step as well, all while the link chains connecting the shaft through back-band to straddle to hames would go clink clink.

Horse getting restless again.

Uncle would say to me be a good lad, go and get the nose Bag:'

We always bring a nose bag, its a great thing to keep a working horse happy, better still if you have a few apple trees growing, nothing compares to a fistful of ripe apples among the oats in a nosebag, what a happy horse, Uncle knows all the tricks.

With the cart all loaded up and well tied down we made our way back to the farmyard, where the load of furze was unloaded onto a flagstone area near the furze chopper, a machine used for chopping it up, making it easier for any horse to consume.

Uncle would say; that brake would make a nice field if it

was reclaimed, and all the roots dug out and get it re-seeded but he was getting older and that's a lot of work, I've enough to do minding the fields I have.
Uncle is not a greedy man, he has time to stop and chat with anyone, but no sooner would the chat begin and Uncle would twist it to the land, what sort of earth do ye have "will ya tell me."
Jakurs he would say I saw a field being ploughed the other day on my home from Dunmanway,
and twas the natest piece of earth I ever laid eyes on. lovely rich red earth, sure didn't I stop and feel it, " I tell ya twas a " gasge " .
Uncle was a great ploughman he could hold his own with any man when he was in his prime, a fact recognised by neighbours all and sundry.
Uncle never boasted about himself.'
Well perhaps when playing cards; something he really loved, you'd have to be crafty to beat some of the
-45- card game players.
Boasting about what cards you would have in your hand may help you to win, but if you don't have the cards to begin with, at best the hope is for a mistake, allowing a win against all possible odds.
Uncle being the only father I know, and he is making me wise at a very early age, willing to share all his knowledge with me.
I am truly blessed:
It's a damp muggy day in summer, a great time for

thinning root crops, as the ground is wet and soggy,
during this sort of weather its very easy to pull up
the weeds that grow around the turnips, mangols,
parsnips, carrots, onions, and cabbage.
So off to the field where the horses are grazing I go.
" Kitty kitt"
I call out as I make a clicking sound with my tongue off
the roof of my mouth , both horses come running up to
me as I wait at the gate.
A pungent smell of horse sweat combined with the damp
mist is wafting thru the air.
I have something here for you kitty I would say, holding
out a piece of turnip of maybe a carrot.
Kitty loved little teats such as these, and would be your
slave for the day.!
Now I walk her back by her mane to the farm yard, as she
is too wet to ride.:
The tackling up is next,
so after I have all the tackling of the harness, I back her
into the dung butt, a dirty old horse cart used for jobs
such as this.
Today Uncle and myself will be thinning a field of
turnips, we will also be weeding as we proceed, and we
also have brought a couple bags of potash to spread on
the drills as we go.;.
Kitty will stand all day as we move from drill to drill, she
follows us up and down the field as we move.
Half way thru the day its time for tea, we have come

prepared for this event.
Thick slices of brown bread,
some cured bacon, and whisky bottles of tea,
stuffed into old woollen stockings.
The tea by now is almost cold, but we are hungry so there is no complaint there:'
While we eat, Kitty is untackled,
and taken for water, then she is allowed to graze of the side of the field, chewing overgrown grass clumps and other shrubbery that grow wildly on the ditches..
Then its back to work,
by end of evening most of the 3 acre field will have been thinned, ifits not finished;
Tomorrows weather is forecast to be the same, so by then it will surely be finished.
" done and dusted "
Back in the farmyard kitty is untackled once again, a few buckets of water thrown over her, and she is given a quick rub down.
then back to the field where she can graze to her hearts content.
So far its been an ordinary days work, with lots more to be done before the day is ended.
Uncle would be rather wet but would continue working, this of course was the reason for his aches and pains, always complaining about stiffness.
Dinner would be late today, and after dinner it is back to

work,
Stalls, piggerys and stables all had to cleaned and re-bed-ed for the night ahead, the farmyard is the centre of farm life.
Our house in Clodagh, faced southwards over looking hills valleys stretching far out over the rolling hills of West Cork
A few fields above our house on a clear day you could see what appeared to be eternity.
Reality is always close by, and the smell of all the dung heaps which grows higher and higher by the day, is situated only a few yards from the front door.
During hot weather the stench is unbearable, we try not to think about it.
But a consoling feature all the same.
A farmers work is never done, even if the work that must be done is complete, just look around and there is so much more that needs to done.
Uncle would check the fatness of the pigs, they would grunt and groan as they scattered about the piggery when he walks among them.
Their moistened curling noses, their pinkish white skin and ring liked tails, shoving and pushing each other toward the circular trough in the middle of the pig house floor;
Some of are strong enough to lift it up the trough with their snouts.
But mostly they play with a big tree branch which keeps

them occupied.
They all have rings on their noses to prevent them from fighting with each other.
It's a very hot strong acrid smell in a piggery.
" even so".
They have their own way, our piggery is on two levels, one is raised about three inches above the other, the upper one for sleeping, the lower level is used for feeding and shitting,.
" What a mess that is "
Getting in among them while trying to clean it out is an experience, they grunt at you, push up against you, always looking for food,
And when you have the chore done.
Its time for some cabbage, a head of cabbage a piece is thrown over the half door, then there is a almighty rush to get at it.
This calms them down until their evening meal of crushed corn and separated milk;
You would have to be there to truly appreciate these animals, they are cunning and intelligent, so much so that they make dogs appear as fools and idiots in the animal kingdom.
Over the piggery is a loft, this is where the corn is kept, the corn lays there on a wooden floor,
the corn has to be turned over and over every two months to avoid fungus growing on the grain.;
This two story building was originally a dwelling house

for humans many years ago.
Underneath its eaves, are several cone shaped mud nests. Swallows unused nest's. They have been coming here for years, and when the weather gets warm, it will be "swallow flying" so busy;
Flag stone step stairs gives access to the high corn loft. Now from time to time when a travelling farm worker comes to earn some money during harvest time, here is where he will sleep.
The bed would be very simple just two huge bran bags filled with straw, a few old ould blankets which he would throw over himself.
Sometimes the overly dry lime stone rendering between the latt's attached to the rafters will be falling out of his hair in the morning as he sits down at the table to eat his breakfast with us.
Then one time, it was a very stormy night, outside the wind is howling its raining very heavy,
" so so dark "
Uncle is waking me from my sleep,
" mo gile "
meaning.; geailge for little helper.
He say's I need you up on the loft roof, I'm very afraid the roof will be blown away with the strong winds.
The trees surrounding the house are bending and shaking, we hear a cracking sound,
at the back of the piggery/loft a huge tree is about to come crashing to the ground, and in a flash its down.

Crows nests are scattered all around,
the cawing of the evicted crows mixes up with the howling winds, coupled with the barking scared dogs. it's a horror story.
Uncle gets a long ladder, I climb up and stretch myself across the slates so as not to slip, if I fall it could be death, definitely serious injury.
Uncle gets a bucket and shovel, fills the bucket with soft fresh cowshit without straw, he brings it up the ladder to me,
" mo gile he say's ".
Every time the wind lifts up a slate I want you to place a fist of cowshit under it and push the lifted slate down into the shit.
The wind keeps howling the rain is falling, now and then when a gust comes along I see several slates lifting, it becomes a crossword puzzle of noughts and crosses, slates that are firm and slates held with cowshit.
About an three quarters of an hour later Uncle tells me I can come down now,.
He helps me down as I seem to have lost my balance from my body being outstretched across the roof.
Back indoors we wash up in the enamel dish, the kettle is boiling, and before going back to bed we have some sweet cake and tea.
Tell ya what...?
little man he says to me, you don't have to go to school tomorrow, I am trilled at the thought,.

I love learning, but I hate school:'
I hate being beaten for stupid simple things, things that Uncle overlooks.
I used to wish that he could read and write and perhaps he could be my teacher, but alas its not to be.
Curled up in my bed I know I will be allowed to stay in bed later than usual.
So its time to do some reading under the blankets with my bicycle flash lamp on my shoulders illuminating the pages of my favourite book;
A cowboy story by Lois Lamour.
Morning "comes" its not easy to sleep.
Cows bawling dogs barking, a whole plethora of farmyard sounds.
An orchestration of nature.
Its another day in the farm of unending work and toil, but Uncle loves his land, he loves his cattle, its not work to him, its not a chore, its his life, and to his farm he gives his life willingly.
Every day begins for Uncle, rising early as usual, then with his working clothes on.'
A dash of water from the barrel across his weather beaten face, and he is ready for the day and all the trials it may bring.
The daily routine of milking cows begins again, the storm has died down, the farmyard is covered in leaves and broken branches twigs and tree remnants from the night before;

Uncle takes it all in his stride.
When taking three bulls to the village, where upon the appointed day, the inspector comes.
 "he and only he"
decides " who is bull among bulls".
Uncle walks through the yard, his wellies with the tops turned down, so as not to give him ire, a problem with the sharp edge of the wellie top.
These wellies have seen better times, and Uncle could do with a new pair, but as he always keeps saying,
" Wilful waste makes woeful want "
So he will wear them out, until the sole is holed, bust or cracked.
The turned down wellie tops of two inches are all black and brown, from milk that sprayed across them, and from the spattered manure being spread on the fields by pike;
This is a hard piece of work and backbreaking;
Curled and crinkled from wear and tear,
ah sure they'll last another month or two, then I'll look good with new wan's when we have the trashing:
As Uncle trawls across the yard to the scalded milk churns with each bucket of fresh milk,
he bends down and picks up the twigs and broken tree bits that are scattered all around.
T'would break ones heart,
he murmurs to himself under his breath, bloody wind rain and storms:
"Aimn an Dia" what was the man upstairs thinking when

he made the world.
What a nate operation we'd have, if we had rain when we wanted it, and sunshine when t'was needed. But I suppose he has his own plan, and all we can do is get on with it.
Every year,
year in year out,
The rota of events never changes;
It is always the same with the exception of a few variables.
A roll over of animals, by the way each animal has a different personality, so what may have worked last year, now has to be altered to suit the animals requirements.!
On a farm you would have cows for about 20 years, for horses, say; about (25 to 27 years) the last few years of a horses life would be spent grazing with no work.!
They are getting old and feeble, having given their life to the farmer and his land:
New horse's now coming on stream, have to be trained into the different modes of work, usually trained alongside an older horse,
to break them in so to speak.
This is a huge challenge for any farmer, if the new gelding or mare has a lot of spirit, its not an easy task.
Different farmers have a handed down way of getting on top of this issue.
From the introduction of the bridle and a single reins,

getting the animal to run around in circles, giving praise and reward, you can get the horse to obey quickly.
Then the trick is to introduce the animal to the winkers, "(a bridle with large leather flaps that prevents the horse from seeing at the side. limiting its vision, to only straight ahead)".
If its harrowing time, witch is always after ploughing, its an ideal way of introducing the young horse to the harrow,
its light for the animal to pull and you can get the horse used to commands,
also get it to draw the harrow up and down the field in straight lines.
Very soon it will be time to tackle it up to a horse cart, not too long after that, its life for the next 22 years or so, are mapped out.!
Frost is the welcome feature when ploughing is about to begin:'
Uncle would take out two well fed horses to a field, tackle them up to the plough and begin the ploughing.
A headland was the start, it's a straight line furrow after this all the other furrows would follow suit, now a ploughman job is hard work, it's a sort of multi task job.
Controlling the horses, watching their temperament, keeping the furrow line equal and straight,
watching out for the saddle board of the plough as the sod of earth is turned over in a wave like motion.
All around are birds hovering overhead waiting for the

fresh ground to open up, revealing a banquet feast of food,.
During February and March, when most of the ploughing is done,
I love to sit and watch Uncle as he urges his horses along the tried and trusted straight lines, see the clay being turned over, its flesh-like rippling earthy seams falling apart;
Revealing a beautiful brown shining colour beset by speckled wet pebbles and stones, diamond like appearance in the frosty clear air of spring, and
in the distance behind, I see the snow capped mountain of Eoin hill;
as it is know locally, its a picture akin to a pastel of colour.
Brown clay green grass,
white topped mountain
blue skies, the odd cloud drifting.
Underneath the old farmer toiling his days on earth away, feeding the nation, loving his land caring for his animals, praising his boy, and giving thanks to the Lord.
Soon all the ploughing will be complete, while we wait for more cold hardy weather to break the now brittle clay up, then the harrowing will begin, followed by manure spreading.,
Christmas has come and gone, the long nights are getting shorter, a new day and year of life is about to begin;
Easter is on the way, it always follows Lent, a time of

immense prayerful devotion.
Hell on earth for all sinners is being predicted by the visiting missionary's .
In the village are two wooden stalls, selling all sorts of religious paraphernalia,
rosary beads,
statue images of the Blessed Virgin, the Sacred Heart, all and every saint, since they invented saints that you can imagine.
Life for Uncle is tough at this time of year, he must find extra strength to comply with all his work on the farm, and the time he has to put to one side for God.
There is a fear among each and everyone, as the priests thump a dogma of endless fire and brimstone into our hearts.
During lent fasting, prayers, and novenas are the norm; its considered to be the duty of every god fearing person, rather than risk the wrath displeasure and curse of god.
Abstaining from alcohol and any earthly pleasure will according to the priests,
bring us closer to our maker on the final day,
a day when we hope to receive our deserved redemption.
Then scene being set, the village is decorated, papal buntings stung across the street,
Every shop window sparkling, full of statues resembling an altar of some sort.
Even private houses are not exempt: all are under the pressure of compliance with catholic church rule.

One could be cursed for eternity
The high point of lent is holy week, a long drawn out affair, masses, devotions, and endless streams of soul searching;
Highest point is " Good Friday "
today is the day to celebrate the death of Christ,.
I am asking myself in a private inner way. Is it correct to do such a thing.
The fervour of the people in constant and endless prayer, processional lines adoring plaster and wood stations of the cross;
Elderly ladies observing the congregation to see if its being carried out in the required and revered devoted way.
Every catholic is obliged to observe today, very little work will be done, farmers get an absolution to do the bare minimum, " ie "
The exception, milking cows feeding livestock, certainly no land work will take place,
if one was to redden the earth today....?
Undertaking such a foolhardy task will result in being blacklisted by neighbours townsfolk and priests alike.
So whether the people believed or not, they must be seen to comply.!
Easter Saturday comes,
its breakfast time, hunger from yesterday is being satisfied, but its not over yet, tonight we will all attend church again.

More devotions, preceded by confession, and ending in Benediction.
The women in their head scarf's and hats are all at one side of the church with their children,
while the men occupy the other side,
In church men and women never mix.
When benediction is over the women and children remain on,
some seeking help from the priests, in the form of blessings and private petitions.
Indulgences are being sold like pigs at the fair, and are quickly snapped up by richer people who can avail of such a luxury, this according the church will allow them easy access to a seat in heaven beside Jesus Christ;
" When they or family members die ".
It has finally arrived Easter Sunday, that is, a day of days in the catholic church, the other exception being Christmas day.
We all get up early, but the sun has been up before us, Uncle used always tell me that if I was up before the sunrise I would be able to see the sun dancing in the sky, it is a belief held by many.
But its water for breakfast, as we are all in a state of grace, and unable and not allowed to eat before we take holy communion.
One of the nice things about today is a feeling of relief that's its all over,
well until next year,

The mass today itself is not as long as the palm Sunday
mass when people are fainting due to the long extended
event.
The church looks resplendent, a scent of incense, and
beautiful flowers,
the congregation are dressed in the very best clothes they
have,.
The entire church receives holy communion, a long
almost unending trail of people piously folding bead
dripped extending hands.
They kneel at the altar rail, their eyes closed, their
mouths they open wide,
awaiting their redeemer;
Meanwhile the choir is singing liturgical hymns
being conducted by an equally pious conductor;
Who when she is not conducting, is terrorising and
torturing the children under her care, as she goes about
her job as a teacher.
(sad memories)...why...?
Meanwhile down in the village after mass, the men have
quietly slipped into the bars for a few pints of porter.
While their women folk are busy doing shopping for the
week ahead, children get the promised treat of a life time,
a six penny wafer ice cream:
But this quick burst of pleasure is only a short
experience as the men soon come out of the bars and
along with the women and children, make their way
home together as a family;

No sooner home, all the nice clothes are replaced by regular daily wear,
we all sit down to the dinner, breakfast having being scrapped for today.
We begin by eating boiled eggs, expected is to be able to consume six hard boiled eggs,.
The main course would be sheep, or mutton as its called. This would have been roasting in the oven or in a bastiable, depending on the household circumstances.
Now we all full up, its time to go out hunting, the dogs are not fed too well today, hunger gives them some venom.
The instinct takes over, we just follow as a terrier begins the fight,
running down into burrows we can hear the screams of the rabbits as the terrier snaps and bites the trapped rabbits,.
Meanwhile on the outside of the burrow, all the larger dogs are getting very anxious,
frantic to join the fight,
With their paws they begin ripping the soil around the entrance to the burrow,
eventually getting to the lair itself, all of a sudden some rabbits run off and are now being chased by a hound or two,
we all get excited just looking at the speed of the hound as they almost fly in pursuit.
The other dogs and terriers make quick work of the rest

of the trapped rabbits.
Its an entire family of rabbits wiped out,
dogs boys and men have had their fun.
Supper will be soon.
The weather is really nice the days are long and very warm, there is a heavenly scent wafting across the countryside, as life is coming into bloom.!
Its hay cutting time.
On this beautiful early summer's day the first of the winter fodder crop will begin its eventful journey to the hay shed, The field from which it is cut is an abundant store of life in the grass.
First Uncle will survey the field from the ditches and fences surrounding, then start the chore itself, the tools for today's work are simple, he brings his scythe edging stone and a two pronged pike.
Today I will be induced to the art of using a pike, and as Uncle cuts a swarth of hay opening up a track all around the edge of the field, I will try and maintain a nice even flow as I move the swarth away from the hayfield.
We are I feel a team of two, as we progress around the field.
When ever Uncle stops to have a smoke, I try out the scythe, its not easy, I'm not strong enough yet.
Tomorrow and the day after will see the end of the beginning of preparations for hay.
When the horses and the mower move in, the event will become alive, lush green tall straight standing grass will

come falling down, wave after wave until symmetric lines of cut hay are stretched all across the field.
While this is unfolding frogs are jumping like crazy, getting away from the ever increasing noise of the mechanical mower.
Uncle gently taps and urges the horse up and down the field.
A curlew or two take flight with their soft mellow song, other hungry birds are feeding their young, take full advantage of the new feast revealing its self before their eyes.
This meadow which I have seen grow from a bare and barren brown flatness, to a world of life in such a short space of time, its colour of purple clovers, yellow buttercups amidst a sea of silky green, while overhead fly the seed ears of hay dancing in the warm summer breezes:
Rabbits are daring the dogs, openly trying to graze in the sun, they are soon banished, well at least to a different field, sometimes the dogs get a rabbit or two,
and they have a quick and instant dinner between themselves.
The three hay-fields are soon mown down.!
Now we let the sun take over;
Two days time we are back again, this time turning over each swarth revealing its green underbelly,.
Another day or two its time for cocking, it's the part I like:'

With our pike in hand we bundle each swarth towards a point where the cock will be situated.
Two people drawing the hay towards one, who for now is making the cocks.
All three alternate functions.!
When the entire field is cocked, is hay rakeing time.
Every inch of each field is raked up.
The hay shed has been cleared out of last years rubbish, a fire of it burns in the haggard.!
Plumes of pale blue smoke mix with the sweet scented summer breezes, trailing off into the distance. The floor of the shed is brushed and cleaned, and then another place in the haggard is prepared for where a reek of hay will stand.
The reek will be the first cattle fodder to be eaten, then the hay in the hayshed will be used up, that will bring us full circle to next year.
I cant wait for the bringing in of the hay.!
Eventually the day arrives, it's a hot day, not a cloud in the sky, Uncle has tackled up the mare and hay-cart:'
Huge thick long ropes and two hay pikes are all we need to do the job.
Out in the hay field we begin by loading up the first hay cock, I am up in the car taking instructions from Uncle,
" good lad mo gile he repeats",
Move that pike full to the left shoulder of the cart, move that pike full to the back right shoulder, on and so forth.

The hay under my feet is now rising up, I am getting higher and higher, when its about six feet high, Uncle is telling me.
Dance on it mo gile.
In the process I am packing it down compressing the load with the weight of my light body, Uncle then throws up the ropes to me, I drop them over the front of the hay load.
Uncle then proceeds to tie the huge ropes around the front shafts of the hay cart.
I am up on top really enjoying jumping up and down like crazy, all the time Uncle is pulling the ropes with one of his special self tightening rope knots.!
Mo gile he is shouting to me, you'll have to eat more brown bread and put a bit a meat on yer bones, you're still a bit on the light side.
Soon we are leaving the hay field with our first load of hay.
Our load takes up the entire width of the short roadway distance we must travel to the haggard. As we move along the road which is really a boreen, as its not been tarred yet,. we leave a trail of hay sops dangling from the overgrown blooming whitethorn hedges either side of the roadway.
Back in the haggard the hay cart is duly backed into the hay shed, the ropes untied, our hay cart now is half untackled to allow it to tip backwards, wherein the entire load slips off and onto the floor of the hay shed.

Its almost akin to building a huge thick wall, as we work the hay into an ever upwardly increasing rising silver green mound.
Such a process will continue until the hay shed is fully stacked with hay, such a lovely smell.
As we get nearer the roof of the shed the heat of the corrugated iron is hot enough to fry eggs on. Sweat is now dripping off us:
Our horse is wildly swishing her tail at flies landing pitching and annoying her.
Back to the hay field we go;
Its great to be out of the shed.
A beautiful breeze blowing across our wet sweat soaked bodies.
We soon dry up, underneath on the road are our collie dogs, snapping at each other, frustrated by the heat of the sun.
Another few loads, and it will be dinner time, my job will be untackling and taking the horse for water,
accompanied by the dogs, wildly barking as I take the horse to the stream, don't be galloping the mare,
Uncle will insist.
It's a temtation hard to resist for a young boy who used to riding horses bareback. But I know Uncle would know and that would displease him.
When I get to the filed where the stream is , I just let Kitty our mare off by herself, she trots towards the stream by herself, meanwhile I am swinging on a gate

talking to the dogs,
When Kitty has had her fill of water, she begins to graze huge clumps of grass off the hedgerow.
She is playing deaf with me, not responding to my call, I am forced to chase after her, she keeps on moving away from me each time I get close enough to catch her, but I eventually back her into a corner of the field with help of the two collies.
I hope you weren't galloping Kitty says Uncle as I get back to the house for dinner, naw I tell him,
Good lad.
Now the hay shed is full, so now on to the hay reek we go.
Hay reeks are more of a building, than what has happened in the hay shed, the hay must be piled in such a way, that when it rains, the rain falls off towards the ground, when the reek is the required height it is raked and combed in downward strokes, it now looks as though its been groomed and thatched.'
All that remains is the crown, this is the roof of the reek, you need to be able to manipulate the hay resembling a an overhanging hairdo.
That's it.
The hay fields now shaved bare, apart from the remaining white stubble baking in the hot sunlight, are being visited by crows jackdaws and magpies foraging for food.'
Uncle not unlike all his neighbouring farmers is now

praying for rain, this will begin a new cycle of growth and the hayfields will in a short space of time look fertile and green again.

Its mid June, Uncle sees that all his tillage fields of root crops need thinning and earthing, now this is not a favourite chore of mine.

It will require several days of consistent back breaking work on our two knees to get the long damp earthy drills into shape, our knees string tied and wrapped in sack cloth, we move along the ever so long lines of root vegetables thinning the veg, and pulling any and every weed we find.'

As we go small heaps of weeds and roots are piling up between the drills, they must be removed later and placed by the side of the field fence where they will decay and totally rot,.!

Now once again here is Uncle with his single furrow plough and Kitty the mare up and down between the drills pushing healthy organic fresh earth around the newly exposed vegetables.

"Thank God that's over"

One of these days it will be bog work, another set of tough days.

Uncle has two different bogs on his farm, one of the bogs is hairy turf, the other is what he calls sweet black hard turf,' this is the one.

Days working in a bog can be very pleasing, but the work is hard. As usual the morning chores can never be

neglected.
And after they are complete is off we go to the
bog.
Once again with Kitty the trusted one, two collies running alongside us, we make our way to the bog.'
Our tools are simple, we use the hay knife, a flat spade shovel, a four prong pike and a wheelbarrow.
Once there on this mid summer day,
" Solstice is nigh "
Kitty is untackled and allowed to wander and graze, the dogs are at it again chasing rabbits, Uncle spots a hare, mo gile ' look look ' he shouts,
what a gift from god.!
Uncle gets to work, with his shirt sleeves rolled up past his elbows, he tightens up his gallowses.
Begins from where he left off last year.
He makes a huge deep cut with the hay knife, plunging it into the soft uncut turf bank.
Uncle will repeat this, in five spade lines forward;
He has a measure in his head, this man who cannot read or write,
"tis the first car load".
Now getting down to floor of the bog, the turf bank is head high in front of him, Uncle will not cut turf with a slean, I hear him say that's alright for mountain men who only have hard ould hairy turf.
Now he removes the first sod off the top, which is quickly discarded.'

Turf cutting begins in earnest at this moment:
Edging the shovel brings the result, he slaps the shovel side through the turf, its like a razor blade going through butter, then he slides the shovel four inches deep into the turf bank,
and in a swinging motion throws the first real sod up on to the dry bank.
A pile is rising, mo gile Uncle calls me towards him, I am playing with the dogs, " be a good lad " pike that pile into the barrow, and spread it all out in flat lines.
We'll make a bog man outa ya yet.'
The empty wooden barrow is heavy to push, and really heavy when loaded up with wet soggy peat, the four prong pike pierces the turf like a fork going through an overboiled brussel sprout.
Surely I am getting my piece of action, its not easy, Uncle is telling me don't fill it so much, use the barrow, small amounts at the time.
The bog is now getting polka dotted.
The days moves on, we break for tea, we have a fine lot of food brought with us, brown bread butter, meat, cheese and blackberry jam to satisfy the sweet tooth.
Its great at this moment, I gather some dry dead wood, Uncle can I light the fire, he hands me the matches, put much more dry grass under the wood, then you'll have a fire.'
He is right.
The fire takes off real well, I get the kettle we have

brought, and go to a stream that's running not far from the bog, with the kettle filled up I get back to Uncle, he is seated on one of the side boards of the horse cart, he is using this as a seat, with his pipe in his hand, a spit from his mouth, make the tripod now he says.
Its my first time hearing the word, "I don't know Uncle" what do you mean, he is laughing, you've a long road to go says he.
Get me three nice long strong sticks, I run to the nearest fence and break off three long twig like sticks, running back as fast as I can.,
will do these do Uncle, grand job altogether;
I still don't know what he going to do, but its so simple. Uncle just sticks them into the ground, pulls them together at the top by tying a small piece of string around them.
Here is where we hang the kettle he laughs, smoke coming out from his mouth and flared nostrils, get some more dry wood mo gile.
" Something about a fire " I am really enjoying watching the kettle as it boils, pushing new bits of deadwood among the fast dwindling fire,.
With the kettle boiled, its tea time, a fine large teapot of tea, while we are now waiting for it to draw.
We crack open a few hard boiled eggs, a grain or two of salt and they too disappear.!
The dogs are excited, they will get the crumbs, and whatever is left over when we are finished.

Its back to work, today and for the next three or four days, until the quota of turf is cut and stretched across the bog;
With the sun beaming down; by this time next week we will be turning the sods over, and if the weather holds up stooking will begin.
Uncle never made a reek of turf in the bog, it was always straight from the stook's to the haggard, why waste time making a reek in the bog and then another reek when its brought home..?
Uncle would burn the upper bog during march, it then would re-grow becoming really green, as he would say, tis lovely grazing for young calves, but the lower bog where turf is cut, that is always wild.
Its a flat area, moving clouds and sunshine reflecting off shiny pools of acidic water, scutch tall tough grass that has been regenerating itself over a millennium swaying in the breeze.
Its perimeter is lined with giant purple heather bushes and sharp green spiked furze bushes, displaying their succulent yellow sweet smelling blooms perfuming the wind.!
Uncle is lucky to have a dry set of flag rocks that make a road through to the centre of the bog, these have been laid out here long years ago.
From the huge heap of black turf now baked dry, we load up the cribbed cart, pileing it in as fast as we can throw the sods, bits break off, creating turf dust which is being

carried by the swirling breezes all over the area, and including ourselves,
its in our hair,
down inside our shirts,
stuck into our Wellingtons.
Eventually we have a new piece of architecture in the haggard.
A lovely tall long narrow tube-like reek of turf, its our cooking and heating for the year ahead.
Now that the birds have all their chicks hatched and reared, the overgrown hedges must be trimmed and cut, the fields will have to be walked and checked for unwanted weeds growing, there is a penalty if weeds, such as docks, thistles, rag worth, are discovered growing, it only takes the word of the local sergeant and a court summons;
Also its time to paint the place up.
A new strong yard brush is brought home from the creamery, all the walls around the farmyard are washed any weeds or grasses growing removed, in a few days time it will all look as new.
Whitewashing with white lime, I like painting, I must be clumsy, spatters of whitewash keep splashing into my eyes, I must run and get some fresh water to wash my eyes out;
After the cow houses, stables, piggery, and barn are whitened, as white as snow, the fowl houses "ie" hens, turkeys, chickens, geese and ducks, these are given their

annual.'
Droppings from fowl is a once a year job. big stands on which they roost on each night are scrapped clean and white washed, the foot high mound of droppings on the floor underneath is a hard dry unbreakable cake.
The outside of the fowl house's are treated to a coat of black tar, preserving their wooden walls from winter weather.
After all that, its now the hay shed that has to get it touch up.
Coming and going to school I see the change.
The nature intended shaped fields begin swelling up, recently they have become a display of what it is they really are.!
From a point where we can not tell one from the other, we now can plainly see their distinctive ears,
the ornate pendant shaped corn ear, compared to the bristly hairy barley ear.
As they sway in the wind, Uncle would remind me to view the hand of god as he called it.
See what happens, perhaps its his breath he would tell me.
Either ways harvest is on the way.
But not before the spuds have to be seen to. they have already been earthed and manured twice, now it's the fear of blight,
"We all remember the famine".
Uncle waits for a dry day.

Made to measure is today, not a breeze and it's a dull cloudy day, perfect for spraying.
Again Kitty is tackled, we load up four 45 gallon barrels onto the horse cart and head off to the river for water, All the wells are now rather dry, just enough for our drinking water.
The fast flowing river water is brown in colour, containing lots of iron content and perhaps the run off acidic water of the nearby mountain as well.
When we have bucketed the barrels as full as possible we take an easy trip to the potato field.
Now here in the potato field, Kitty is un-tackled while we prop the shafts so as not to spill any water.'
Uncle then pours the blue anti blight powder substance "bluestone" into the water filled barrels.
He is stirring and stirring, until he gets the mixture an deep blue texture, ah that's good bluestone he would be saying to me.!
The portable brass spraying machine which has been washed and scrubbed is now back in action, having been idle since this time last year.
It takes three gallons to fill it to the top, Uncle places the sprayer on the horse cart, I am up on top with a large jug filling the sprayer each time he comes back for a fill-up.
As time wears on Uncle is getting bluer, as if a huge bottle of ink has been showered on to him:
I see him disappearing from view, pumping the sprayer as he traverses among the huge halums of potato stalks,

a fine blue mist is all I can see.
We have three acres of potatoes, so it's a one day job of work, but it will require another session later in the season, when the weather becomes damp and muggy perfect for blight conditions.
We don't sell any of this crop, we eat them, the fowl eat them, and of course the pigs love them.'
The back and tailboard of the horse cart is a mess of bluestone,
Uncle's clothes are totally covered in blue, his unshaven silver beard is now sparkling blue to match.
The blue seems hard to remove, but Uncle pays not much attention to it, he goes about the usual daily farmyard chores;
Day in day out;
Never is time really available for any pleasure,
Work work work:
Uncle has been devoted to his farm ever since he was a small boy himself, in his brief tale telling's to me, he recounted when as a young man in his late teens, he was at mass one Sunday morning, the priest made an announcement that the black and tans were on their way to the village.
On the night before, the bridge over the railway line had been demolished, this of course would effect the deployment of troops, all the younger people were given a dispensation and allowed to leave before mass itself was ended.

He tells me how sad it was to watch from a hillside overlooking the village, as the tans forced all the old and infirm people out of the church, and proceeded to make them remove all the rubble from the now shattered railway line. At gunpoint.!
When this was done, they were allowed home;
Later on that evening as the tans drove up and down through all the roads and boreen's around the parish, they passed by Uncles house,
one of his collies ran after the military tender, they just shot the dog for no reason; ah twas an awful time for a man to be living:
I am sitting and listening attentively, Uncle I would ask him will the tans come back again, as he spit out of the side of his mouth, they better not, unless they want an taste of Barry and his men.
Who's Barry I ask Uncle, he is a great man, a hero, you are a good little singer, you must learn the boys of Kilmichael, then you will know who Barry is.'
I really enjoy when Uncle and me would be going out for litter, we would be travelling leisurely towards where the rushes grow.
Uncle would bring the local newspaper "southern star" Tucked underneath his seat the straw filled branbag, he would pull it out and hand it to me, read me that he would say.
I begin reading, "no not that", go to the auctions, there is a section in the paper that carries all the farm auctions

and whatever else is being sold.
I find myself reading to him, I am coming across words I can pronounce but don't understand, and its great because Uncle tells me what they are, a " whittletree ", What is that, ah yes says Uncle.'
Its what's used connect two horse to a plough, how much do they want for it, I don't know, its states, to be sold in lots or separate:
Roll on he says, I keep on reading and reading, I love reading, we get to the field of rushes, well now its back to the grind stone.'
Uncle cuts swarth after swarth of rushes, as I place them on the cart.
He says that's enough, read out another few auctions to me mo gile.
He takes a plug of Mick McQuade tobacco out of his waistcoat pocket, cuts off small small chunks, and rolls them feverously between his huge hands, all the while listening and correcting me if I get the words wrong, tis great stuff he says, being able to read, I wish I could do it, but tis too late now, as he strikes a match and lights his pipe.
We get back to the farmyard, the litter is just tipped out in a heap;
We wont be needing litter much longer, as we will be having straw after the trashing.
The fields are turning a deeper shade of gold day by day
The corn barley and wheat fields are being prepared,

swarths all around the perimeter having being removed, now we wait for the mowing machine.
The day comes, the horse is once again tackled to the mower, it's a tricky job mowing.
A lot of co-ordination is needed;
One must control the horse, while each four to five feet a lever is manually manoeuvred, creating a bundle of straw, this will then be taken by hand and manipulated into a sheaf, sheaf making is an art form itself,
one must, while holding the bundle of straw together make a binder out of a clump of strands of the straw to tie and hold the sheaf together.'
When the field has all been sheaved.!
Its stooking time, and one by one the stooks appear as if by magic,
these tall golden six sheaf pyramids.
When the last of the corn, barley, and wheat fields are harvested and stooked, the stacking will begin, at this point all the stooks will be drawn to an area where small round tall stacks will arise.
The stacks will remain in place until they are drawn into the haggard for trashing, this is the highlight of the farm year.
The Meitheal. " community working together"
In the meantime Uncle's regular daily farm work goes on unabated.
Cows are calving and must be given attention, the young calves will be bucket fed for a few days, after that they are

led out to the fields where the hay had been growing,
here they can familiarise their palette with the sweet new grass.'
Its August, another year is flying by, there is talk about the humid damp weather,
Thunder and lightening is scaring the animals,
sometimes when they get frightened, they can run for miles.
It's a big job of work rounding up scared cattle, and separating out the neighbours cattle, who are now grazing on our land;
Uncle is good at this,
he seems to know everyone's cows, calves, and almost every animal, down to the dogs and cats.
With the thrashing's fast approaching, each farmer is doing at his own preparations.
Its busy busy busy, Dawn to dusk.'
Between now and the thrashing's, say's Uncle to me one day as I arrive home from school, we will replace the footpath leading to the cow houses.
Its great, another few days off school.'
The pathway outside the cow byres are paved with huge long narrow flag stones, these stones are here a long time, and periodically need underpinning.
They are very heavy, but with the aid of a crowbar can be shifted and turned over.!
Underneath is a setting of grey clay and gravel mixed, but over time with rainfall, plus urine from the cows, all

the grey bonding clay simply disappears, so off to a river bed at the end of our farm, where this grey clay is in abundance.
This is a really tough job of work, the clay is lodged at the side of the river bank.
With a pickaxe and shovel Uncle breaks open a tract, I in turn have to shovel it onto the horse cart.
We really don't need a lot, just two cart loads, then we gotta get to a gravel pit for a few cart loads of pebble gravel.
Once we have assembled the items, its easy peasy.
Once we have laid down the clay and gravel mix, we just lay the huge oblong flag stones edge to edge, the weight of the cows will do the rest, is a few days all is neat and flat again.
Its nearly time to draw in the corn, and when dry days appear, Uncle takes advantage, With our horse cart out in the fields, Uncle on the horse cart laying our the sheaves of corn, as this is a job beyond me as of yet, and time is precious.
I today am the piker, up on the top of the stack out in the cornfield I am, pikeing sheave after sheave down to Uncle, soon I am sinking, while all the time he is rising, and its getting harder for me, my hands are blistered from the pike.'
We trudge along the boreen back to the haggard, and now we must make the huge tall stacks.
Stack making is another art form, beginning with a stook

of six sheaves, then a ring of sheaves in a very large
circle, soon it will be rising skywards, as the piker pikes
up sheave after sheave, sleep will come easy after a day of
pikeing, sore arms and a sore back.
We now have eight huge tall stacks in the haggard, there
they will remain until the thrashing day arrives.
For many days to come, like several more farmers Uncle
will be missing;
Once he has all the morning chores put away, Uncle will
be off to whatever farmer is having a thrashing:
Then his turn will come.
So it does, but not before all the preparations, the food,
the porter, required to feed all the men folk that will
arrive to do the job.
It is a community effort.!
You can hear the whining of a tractor along the road in
the distance, as it pulls the thrashing machine, and also
behind it is a conveyor belt piker, this is used to pike the
straw up on to a huge reek of straw that will begin
arising, once the thrashing begins;
Men are sitting around talking and waiting, more are
smoking pipes, some are just standing with their elbows
crossed over their pikes, every man brings a pike, they
are all ready to give a good hard days work, not a penny
changes hand.
The machinery arrives, it's a almighty effort getting the
thrasher and piker located properly, sure enough
everything becomes assembled;'

With the thrasher now between the stacks of corn and barley, the tractor is a short distance away from it, connected by a huge long canvas belt which turns the thrasher, causing the entire machine to work;.
We are about to begin, everyone knows their place
Blue TVO smoke is rising from the tractor's exhaust, as the thrashing man is revving up an down the his engine, he is making sure all is well.
The man doing the drum feeding is in his box, surrounded by young boys, sharp penknives in hand ready to do sheaf cutting of the binders.
On top of the stacks are fit men awaiting to begin pikeing sheaf's on to the thrasher, down below at the back are another two men, they will be very busy soon when the grain comes pouring out from four chutes down into the jute string bags.
At the front of the thrasher, the piker is located and connected, its conveyor motion takes the dripping straw upwards and it drops down onto the men making the reek.
As the bags fills up, other men are carrying bags of grain on their back to the barn, soon the barn will be full, now they must make a "sugan" a straw round storage stack for holding grain.
Huge fat straw ropes are made from the freshly thrashed corn, and laid one on top of the other, until it resembles a grain silo.
These will soon be full, then they will have to be topped

with a thatched roof of straw.
Every now and then the chaff has to be removed, the corn is thrashed first, then the barley, about two hours into the event a break for a few bowls of porter, then straight back to work, when almost two thirds is complete, it will be time for dinner.
During dinner time Uncle will be busy helping out with the thrashing man as he goes about checking his machines,
all must be well oiled before we begin again.
Nightfall is moving in fast, the pace of work has slowed down considerably, the men are getting drunk from all the porter, not to mention the potcheen that someone always brings along;
We are now working by the lights from the tractor, here and there about the haggard you will find tilly lamps and storm lanterns lighting up the footpaths to the barns and the farm house.
The day has ended, the machinery is all being dismantled and checked out, tomorrow is another days work for the thrashing man.
Most of the men congregate inside the farmhouse, where a singsong develops, Uncle not to be outdone in his own house, shouts to me to sing your new song,
The Boys Of Kilmichael,
and every time I get to the chorus, I am drowned out, as they all join in.
You're a great young fella, you'll be a mighty man when

you grow up, they nod in agreement with each other, sure you might join the IRA.
Take out your melodeon says Uncle and give us a blast, I have this new accordion, I don't know many tunes yet, but I am sitting with two drunk men on either side humming tunes into my ears,!.
It goes this way young fella, diddlie diddlie diddlie.
Naw shouts the man on my other side. It goes diddlie diddlie diddlie.
They both have two different versions of the same tune all very confusing.
Soon its getting late ,they begin to disappear one by one, they all know its another day of trashing in another man's farmyard tomorrow.
I get another day off school " because ",.
I have to tidy up the haggard today, chaff is all over the place, I brush and rake until I get it in a heap.
Then I move in bagfuls to the hen houses, and the chicken house where I spread it out, it becomes a base for their droppings.
All the way to the barn is a trail of grain, it has to be gathered and brushed up. It will be then scattered to the hens in the yard, and quickly devoured.'
Uncle is missing most days now after he returns from the creamery,.
He is working for the same men who worked for him, each farmer helps out his neighbours, get a day give a day.!

If the thrashings are local, and I am home in time from school, I will be on my way helping out, I will be getting some of the lovely red lemonade, those long necked bottles of " Little Norah ".
It sure happened fast, all the thrashings are now finished the winter is drawing near, days shorter and shorter, at least now as many cows to milk in the morning, as the majority are in-calf.
Now that those hard working boozey thrashing days are over for this year.!
Back to the grinding stone.' the root crop now must be harvested, first will be the " spuds, poppies, praties, potatoes" what ever the name.
Their gallant proud halum of stalks now a crumbled mass of brown dusty fibre filled rubbish, duly collected and burned, as the smoke drifts across the potato field, Uncle is out with his horse and his single furrow plough up and down through the drills, splitting them open as he goes.
Behind him here I am gathering the biggest of the crop bucket by bucket until all the bags are full, then its on to the small spuds, they will be used as pig fodder.'
When all potatoes are dug out and bagged, we will then bring them home by the cart load:'
Beside the barn behind the piggery, we have a small plot of ground, here will lie all the root crops, spread out among the pits that are now being prepared.
The potato pits are firstly lined with straw, and when the

pit is full, the mound of potatoes will be lovingly dressed in straw, and finally covered in clay.
Once the potatoes are harvested and pitted, then we spend the next two weeks harvesting the remaining crop. The turnips, mangols, carrots, parsnips, each root will occupy its own pitted domain.!
The dung butt horse cart will for now have its first clean out of the year:'
Seemly it goes on forever.
Now all the machinery used over the past year needs a seeing to.
The ploughs, harrows, rollers, mowing machines, and all the hand held implements need checking cleaning and an oiling, most likely a trip to the forge to repair any damage occurred during the season past.
Uncle takes time to walk his land, he is a proud man, I am very happy walking along side him, as he checks the fence's, ditches and gaps leading to each and every field of his farm.
All that remains now is cleaning out the chimney, our chimney it a mass of soot, we have a very large fireplace, look up through the chimney breast you can see the sky and some tree tops swaying in the wind.
Three or four inches thick tar like soot line the chimney breast wall, this wet soot will dribble down the wall of the chimney every time the rain is heavy.'
Uncle scrapes away the excess soot with a home made scraper, tis clean enough now he say's, once the soot cant

catch fire all will be well.'
Uncle is more interested in touching up his horse cart, it needs a new coat of preserving paint, so armed with a big tin of red lead paint, he sets about renewing the cart, some damaged boards of the wooden cart floor may need replacing.!
It's a time to reflect over the year past, now that we have long nights:'
Back to the scoraoicht.'
Long nights here in Uncles house pass by rather quickly, Scoraiochter's as they are called visit our house to play cards, and when its tea time for a break from playing cards. Invariably one or two of the scoraiochter.s play at being a seanachi.
Evening's of immense pleasure in our kitchen, while the light of the lantern falls upon the kitchen table, the rest of the room is in semi darkness, lit up by the occasional flare-up in the big open fire grate, as sparks shower outwards from the burning ash wood blocks in among the sod's of turf;
During the tale telling of the seanachi, we all listen intently, not wishing to miss a word, he tell us of people returning from the dead, people who been cheated while on this earth.
He really puts the hair on the back of our necks rising, as he recounts story after story, about when spirits of the dead return, taking revenge, spreading disease and trouble among the people who initially brought about its

downfall.
Did ye not notice during the year in so and so's farm, how little grain he had out of those fields, "I tell ye" t'was the spirits that did that.
What else could ensure such a drastic harvest:'
When things get so quite, the only sound is the wind outside howling;
It carries the sound of a fox crying in the distance, there ye have it, " de ye hear " he says, that's the banshee calling, someone is going to die tonight.
Uncle sort of wakes up, he too is taken in by the amazing tale, right says Uncle lets get back to the cards.
On goes the game, penny's changing hands.
I always feel happy when the card playing is over, Uncle say's ,
"mo gile"
play a few tunes on the melodeon, and give us a song, its lovely doing this, I could do it all the days of my life, yeah that's what I wish to do forever and ever.
In the back of my mind is the fear, terrible though it is, I must grin and bear it,.
I know that again tomorrow the beatings, punishments and abuse will continue unabated.
 just cant wait for school to finish, if I had a gun I would shoot the teachers, what is wrong with them, Uncle never gets angry with me, even when I get it all wrong.
He never gets cross with his animals, and they never seem to do his bidding.

Teachers are supposed to be educated and understand everything. Seems as though they just read a few books and are now indoctrinating innocent children to be as they are taught.
Uncaring cruel, bitter, and unloving.
How can we learn in such a climate of fear, afraid to ask for help, we plod along in the knowledge, that what ever we do, it will always be the wrong thing.
I give up.!
Another day off from school, its wonderful, but of course I will do my lessons at home, doing lessons at home is something I love;'
On the final day of school year, we all get our new books for the coming curriculum year, I am excited about new books, I rush home after school.
Take them all out and begin reading,'
History, geography, grammar, my favourites,:'
I read them cover to cover, just great, all these new words it's a continual journey between the books and the dictionary:'
Uncle smilingly would say, be careful your head might swell up with all those books.!
" mo gile " take a break from the books for a few hours come and help me a while, Frank the saw man is coming soon, after the huge storm last night, we have a few trees down.
It's a dry hardy late autumn evening the sun is low in the sky, and sinking fast, Frank arrives with his chain saw,

such new yokes says Uncle, none of us had seen one before.
The trees are spit from their roots upwards, what were once stately sycamore and ash trees now lay fallen, their branches crumbled.'
Frank goes to work, in an hour or so, he has reduced the two trees to a long line of rolls, they resemble slices of swiss roll.
Frank gets his few pounds and heads off to another job, Uncle now begins the job of splitting the big rings into blocks for burning in the fire.
Tomorrow will see the end of this chore.
November is here, its time for religion once again, Devotions, missions to our church, an impending uncertain future and fear of god priests take over the parish.'
Uncle is attending confession, listening to the mission priests,
as they spread the word of god, each man is entitled to his conjugal rights, I hear one say, as I sit along with the other altar boys during a sermon.
What's conjugal rights I ask Uncle, ah wait awhile he says.
" mo gile " you're a long way off that.
It must be one of the mysteries they always refer to during sermons, there are many many mysteries.
Its very cold the weather now, the ground is a white solid frozen glass sheet each morning.

Not a good day for getting those pleasurably dished out slaps of the birch rod, stinging the children's cold cold fingers, as they try to write and do their sums.
The mountain behind our farm is now totally covered in snow.
The wild mountain goats living wild up there during the rest of then year are now coming down to the lower land in search of a meal. we dare not go near them, wild is too soft a word for a mountain goat, especially as accompanying the flock is a huge angry buck goat, and he is very protective of his harem.
As Uncle would say don't draw them on ya.
Feeling liberated at the thought of the missions leaving us, it wont be long now until Christmas.
I look forward to Santa, even though I have reason to believe he is not real;
Sort of like the banshee and ghosts that the seanachi has us told about.
Wrapped up asleep and very cosy in my bed I feel Uncle as he taps me gently, " mo gile " rise and get up, we have a sort of emergency, what's up Uncle, get on your clothes and come down stairs.
I hear someone talking in a very low voice coming from the kitchen, down stairs I come, and here sitting by table is a man I know well, he is a distant cousin of Uncle, good morning to ya little boy he greets me, or is it good night:'
They are drinking tea, when the tea is finished we tackle

up two horses, the dogs are put in an outhouse, so the neighbours wont suspect anything,
we gently walk the horses along the icy road with the whippletree in tow,:'
I am still wondering what's going on.
There stuck at the side of the road is a Morris Minor van capsized over on its side. It seemingly had slipped of the road as the driver negotiated the huge high hill not far from our farmhouse.
The van contained about six wooden casks, full of illegal whisky, "ie" poteen.
Firstly Uncle and his cousin removed the casks one by one, placed them inside the field nearby, just in case anyone may pass by.
We then tied the horses to the morris minor van, and bit by bit managed to pull it free from the dyke that it had lodged itself into.
Reloaded the casks, then Uncle and his cousin sat inside the van drinking samples of the pooten, while I stood on the roadside holding the horses:
As Uncle, horses and me made our way home after our good deed, I want ya to swear that you'll never utter a word of tonight to a soul, swear, come on " mo gile ", will ya swear, yeah:' Uncle I do.
Uncle is still busy even the dept's of winter, the cattle have to be tended to each day, but there is an air of relaxation time to time, the post man will call, Uncle will share a pipe full with him, in between get news of any

thing happening, the post man is as good as any newspaper.
And during Christmas, you will find a very drunk post man, going from house to house delivering letters and parcels, he is most welcome in each and every house that he visits.!
Large glasses of whisky big slices of Christmas cake, you can hear him singing as he makes his way along the roads and boreens.
Parcels from England and America, letters containing money from sons and daughters, those great people who are not forgetting their family at home, and the great almighty link, the famous post man.
This is time of year when turkeys become the currency of the day, they fetch a nice few pounds, but this part of the farm year really belongs to the woman of the house, with this new income, she will be able to do the Christmas shopping.'
Tins of biscuits, Christmas pudding, loads of meat, lots of porter, bottles of whiskey, also some presents for the child.'
It's a three day affair, much too long say's Uncle, one day is enough;
Uncle brings along with him today, he enjoys the 26th of Dec, St Stephens day, and so do I, meeting boys of my own age,' it's a day for the annual trotting races, a big crowd will descend on the village, porter will be drank by the gallon, whisky will disappear like melting the icicles

dangling from the drainpipes:'
When the races are finished and all the money has changed hands, many's the sore head and pocket will be had.
Here and there fights will occur, too much drink, things better left unsaid, now being uttered, and a price will be paid for every word.
Throughout the coming year;' men who were friends in the year past, now almost pass each other by without a glance or a hello:'
" close country living "
There is a funeral taking place to day says Uncle, and funerals can be sensitive;
Here is the common ground, a place to forgive and forget, not always easy, again it could be problems about an inheritance:'
Or some small unresolved argument that may give rise to an unexpected verbal explosion.!
Uncle would sometimes say funerals ain't all there made out to be;
In the church a dead man is a great man, then as he is being laid to rest
Whispers fly about, people are slow to forgive, they never forget;
Whisky is always dished out at the graveyard gate, as people leave the cemetery, a man usually stands at the gate with a small glass, fills it, and hands one glass to every one.

In some cases a glass of sherry would be given to the women folk:'
A well liked man would later be well remembered in the village pubs, a singsong may occur in memory of the dead person.
Revelry may turn to a fight.
Sunday morning mass following the funeral we would be treated to a long sermon regarding the behaviour of funeral goers.
How to respect the dead, and the consequences of not understanding the wrath of god;
I say to every man here to day, if any of you bring the name of our lord into disrepute, you will have hell to pay for your ignorance.
No doubt next Saturday will be a busy confessional outing.
It's a new year, feeling not much different than the one past, Uncles life will take another spin around the sun as he calls it.
Year in year out never a break, no holidays no free days, he has to keep working, he is a slave to the land and all it brings him.
The ice cold weather is now freezing, the cattle are all in their warm stalls, horses in stables, its no wonder that the wonder of the nativity scene is so revered by the country folk. Uncle keeps his animals almost in luxury, and it pays off, he has less call to the Vet.
Soon the frosty weather will abate:'

The ploughing season will be in full swing, the manure spreading, then the ploughing, the harrowing, then the seed planting, and ground rolling, sit back and wait for nature to take its course;

One of these days the stations of the cross will be on the move again, mass will be celebrated in several household all over the parish.'

Each town land will have a designated house, usually read out during the mass, the preparations will begin in earnest, washing painting, getting ready for the stations is a huge event.

The day of the stations is a day when the women rule over all, the house is made as clean and as perfect as it can be, it's a day of extreme reverence.

A showcase of religious piety.

The main living room the kitchen converted into a farm house version of a church, the dinner table has become an altar, its legs having being propped up, raising it higher same as an altar height in church.

Draped in a white bed sheet, which is usually made from discarded flour bags, starched and ironed until its corners become rigid seams.

It is then decorated with vases of flowers, and centre piece will be a crucifix, on either side will be the candlesticks, those reserved for when there is a death in the house.

It's a time of year I love, as an altar boy I get asked by the priest to serve all the stations around my part of the

parish,
Uncle will be saying to me, lad you're so holy now maybe you might become a priest yourself.
And here is another " stations of the cross " about to be celebrated.
The worshippers arrive in dribs and drabs, the women all go inside the house, while the men hang around outside talking in low voices, I have already arrived, and as I have been instructed by the priests, check to see if the altar has all that's needed.
The priest will arrive, all the men hanging outside will remove their hats when he gets out of his car.
On his entrance into the house,
the women folk will almost prostrate themselves, an eerie silence comes over the house, upset only by the clock on the wall with its tick tock, tick tock.
With the arrival of the priest, its as if the Lord has come down from heaven,
people are in awe:'
The priest is led by the woman of the house to the parlour, where she treats him to a few nice shots of whisky.
He then puts on his stole, and invites the assembled crowd to attend confession, one by one each and every body confess their sins.
When confession is over, mass will begin, but not before the priest has another few shots.
With his demure vestment clothed, he makes a grand

entrance from the parlour,
I ring a small bell to signal his entrance, then with a simple blessing of his hands the mass begins.
All is going well until we reach the offertory, there is a large sacred heart statue of Jesus Christ standing in the kitchen window, the priest is raising up the host, and as he does so,'
The head falls off the statue, the priest is in shock, frantically all the women begin praying the rosary in a scream like manner, the priest appeals for calm;'
There has to be an explanation;
On inspection he finds that previously the head had been snapped or broken off, and repaired with glue, which has now come unstuck from the warm sunlight beaming in through the window.'
No no says the priest.! assuring everyone, its not a miracle or a sign from god, let's get back to the mass, he continues on and the mass comes to an end.
It's the talk of the household:'
Now that mass is over its breakfast time, we are all very hungry, having been fasting since last night.
The priest is taken by the woman of the house to the parlour, it's a battle now between those who wish to sit next to the priest.
Usually those who give most in dues.
The parlour table is covered in a linen laced crotchet tablecloth, well polished silver knives, forks, and spoons shine out among the finest crockery, most likely the

china ware had been given as a wedding present to the couple.
Its going to be a fry, on the black range are three frying pans cooking at full blast, soon the rashers, black pudding, and fried eggs will be presented to the rev father.
And as the plates of food make their way to the table, the rev father says grace before meals.
He is sitting in pride of place, buttering his soda bread with carefully butter rolls of homemade butter.
Smiling and appearing pious, all the women around him are being very careful with their words.
I feel an uneasy pressure, as I know all these ladies, but the way they are carrying on today, it seems they have had a brain transplant.!
When the first and most important breakfast sitting is finished, the rev father says grace after meals, excuses himself from the table, we all rise up in unison with him as he makes his way to the kitchen.'
The next sitting will now be fed.!
The priest has now long gone, the conversation topic is about the head of the statue, how it happened, and why did it happen at that very moment:'
Uncle is sitting talking to other men, usually about things on the farm, " mo gile " he says to me run home and get your melodeon give us a few tunes, put a bit a life into the place.
When I arrive back with melodeon tied on the back of my

bicycle, a woman is singing a song, a party is in full swing in the middle of a bright sunny day.
I am seated by the fireplace, I must play some lively tunes now, as they all want to dance.
The day moves forward rather quick. At evening time men folk go home to milk the cows, but when they have done that, they will all arrive back to the party.'
Several more people now arrive at the farmhouse for the party, many of these people are from the other religion, And would not be at the mass.
This party will go on until late into the night, all retiring home by starlight.
We sing our way homewards by starlight, an odd owl flies by on their nightly hunt, their graceful white wings make a flapping sound as they move across the moon in the sky.
 Uncle is up early as usual, we have to trim the horns of a cow, Canister the lead cow, she is a very old cow, now over twenty years of age, she has a horn, which is now growing towards her eye.'
Uncle is very fond of canister, I asked Uncle why is she called canister, just look at her he says, does she not look like a canister, yes I agreed, she sure does;
Canister leads the cows from field to field as they graze for pasture, now we must tie her head on to the large stone separators in the cow byre manger. Then with a sharp saw cut of about two inches of the offending horn, canister shows no tendency to object, all goes well, in

a short space of time problem solved.
Uncle tells me that I must take a day of school because its fair day time again, he has a lot of cattle for sale, bullocks, and springing heifers.
The fair-day comes, up at five in the morning,
Uncle is busy getting ready as I come down stairs, he is sitting on one of the hobs beside the still warm fireplace, putting on his dark brown well oiled hobnailed boots.
Then he laces his gators, pulling the thongs in and out through the gator eyes all the way up to his knees:'
Uncle looks well today, his waistcoat, collarless striped shirt, fastened with a polished brass button.
At the fair he will stand out;
Outside it's a sharp chilly day.
After our breakfast, we have to gather together the heifers and bullocks that will be sold today.
They are full of energy,
Uncles cattle are well fed, separating them in the pre dawn darkness from the others takes a long time.
Eventually we get them out on the boreen, and with our ash plant sticks hunt them along the road in front of us towards the town of the fair.
This is not an easy job, they keep breaking into neighbours land, and getting them back out again is not without its problems.
The dawn is now breaking towards the east, the early morning sun is spreading a little welcome heat:
We struggle with these cattle all along the road until we

get near the town:'
Here we are met by other farmers along the way, who have the same problems as ourselves.
As we draw near the town we are met by some early morning cattle dealers.!
These are the ones to avoid, they do their best to convince to farmers to sell there and then, but Uncle will not hear of it.
They are an intimidating bunch of men.
We continue driving the cattle along the shit sodden street leading to the fair green, where most of the cattle will stand until they are sold.
Dealers walk up and down, checking out the livestock.
The pubs are open since early morning and doing a roaring trade.
As there are no restaurants, some houses open up their parlour's to the farmers and offer tea and sandwiches very cheaply, in the process make a few bob for themselves.
The fair is now in full swing, its a town resounding the bawling of the cows calf's, heifers and bullocks, they are agitated and frightened by the strange and unfamiliar surroundings.
Bit by bit they are all bought up, each dealer has his own colour marker, he places his sign on the rump of every animal he buys.
When mid afternoon comes, we hear the sound of the steam engine as it pulls its train of cattle wagon's into

the railway station.
You can hear the dealers shouting the names of certain men, advising them to bring their cattle to the railway yard;
Once there they will be placed in the cattle wagons, and then the farmer will get his money, but now without the dealer looking for what he calls luck, a sure give me a few more pounds back than that.
These dealers are a wile bunch:'
Up to every trick, back in he fair, deals are still being made, dealers bring some poor farmer in the pub fill him with whisky, then convince him to part with his animals for far less than what they are worth.
But the day is not over yet, now its almost impossible not to tread on any inch of the street that is not covered in cattle shit, its on the walls of the houses, its on the footpaths,
its everywhere, steam rising up, as the cattle shift wearingly around waiting.
Uncle give me a half a crown, I use it buying sweets, I visit the harness maker, I love the smell of leather, he sits in his window observing the days event. Today he will make a lot of money, new orders are placed and old bills paid up in full.
Uncle calls me " mo gile " we are going home now, he has secured a lift by tractor from a man travelling our way, so the two of us hop up on the side wings of his tractor, one of us on either side, as the tractor man brings us the four

miles home, dropping us off not too far away from our farm.
Uncle thanks him, and promises him a reward in future, tis alright, tis alright.
Another time says the man with the tractor.
We arrive home, have our quick meal, and the work starts all over again.
Milking the cows, cleaning out the cow byres, the horse stables, on and on it goes.
Morning comes, its off to school for me, that dreaded place, the only solace I feel is, soon I will be finished with school forever, and not a minute too soon.
When I get home after another day of listening to our teacher ranting and raving, Uncle tells me I must bring two horse's to the forge to be shod.
Another one of my favourite places is the forge, the two brothers who run their forge are real nice men.
They are always covered in filthy black dust from the hot coal fire that's always burning, they do everything in iron.
Men of iron.
Through out the village the clanging sound of the hammers ring out, as they bend and shape the hot red iron into horse shoes.
Gates, railings, and animal feeding troughs.
Anything that can be made from iron is their forte.
Uncle warns me not to gallop the horses, as I have a reputation for riding horses as fast as they can go, so I

will obey him.
Because other farmers along my route will report back to him about my behaviour.!
I arrive at the forge, get off my horse, and tie the two of them to the rail provided.
I now await my turn, I am not the only one with horses to be shod.'
Meanwhile inside the hot forge, the two brothers are working as fast as they can go, horses come in and horses go out, at one side of the forge are long strips of iron, these they place into the fire, I get the pleasure to work the big bellows that fires up the fire.
The handle of the bellows has a huge big bull horn on its end, the sparks start to fly as the iron heats up, its then taken and an appropriate length sheared off, this will form a horse shoe, but a lot of work still needs to be done before its complete.
The blacksmith now bends it around the anvil, swinging his hammer with his large sinewy arms, his steel like muscles rippling, pink lines appearing across his brow, as sweat drips off his black dusty face.
When he has a shape that resembles the horse's hoof, he begins to punch small holes to accommodate the shoe nails that will hold it on to the horse's hoof.
Meanwhile his brother, is perched underneath the horse's belly, with the horse's leg between his own legs, pincers in hand removing the old worn out shoes, then with a razor sharp curled knife he trims the horse's hoof

growth.

The red hot iron shoe is then placed against the newly shorn hoof, an imprint is made amongst a cloud of smoke coming from the burning hoof, it's a smell of burning flesh, awful.

The hoof is now pared to the imprint, this is repeated on each leg.

A circular hole is then cut out on the tail-end of each shoe, this is where the frost stud will be placed.

When all four are done the job is complete.

Of course I have brought a nose bag.?
this will keep the horse's placid while they await their turn.

Once its over, the horse's cant wait to get back home and out to pasture.

How did it go asks Uncle, was there many in front of you, a few I said. Ah sure there's always someone needing things, tis the way of the world.

I am now ten years living with Uncle, and going on almost fourteen years of age, I have learned a lot from him, some may be of no use in an ever changing world, but as Uncle puts it, knowledge is a light burden to carry around.

Recently Uncle has not been feeling too well, his doctor is advising him to take things easy, sell the farm he was advised, tis breaking my heart I heard him say.

Do you want it he said one day to me when we were out in a field.

Naw I replied, I don't want to be a farmer, why not he insisted, the work is too hard, I want to be a musician, ah sure that for the thinkers, your above that sort of daft stuff.!
I am now able to drive cars tractors, motor bikes, in fact anything that moves.
I go to dances, places I should not be until I am eighteen years of age, I am egged on by neighbours, you're a big man now they say.
Uncle is unaware of my expeditions to dance halls near and far, money is hard to come by, and it seems that all the great friendly neighbours are not really his friends after all.
Some of them approach me to sell them some bags of oats, I get ten shilling a bag.
Stupid I am, but I am being influenced unbeknown to myself.
Praise is heaped upon me, and I fall for it.
Soon I am reduced to thief.
Who's going to find out, our lips are sealed they would say to me.
Uncle is in hospital recovering from an operation,
" poor man "
I don't really know the extent of his anguish, the worry on his mind.
Knowing the love he has for his farm and animals, it must be a huge burden thinking about them.
Uncle comes home from hospital after two weeks, things

have gone amiss in his absence, I am not big or strong enough yet to run the farm.
He has a load of bandaging about his neck, where they removed the growth that had been increasing for quite some time, sore is too soft a word he said to me, when he described his wound, they very nearly cut the head off me.
But I suppose in time twill heal up.
No way on earth I can do the work it takes to keep the farm going, Uncle starts to sell the cattle and the pigs, that at least will reduce the work.
The bandages come off after a week, the local doctor is checking it out, he is not too happy with what he sees and recommends that Uncle has to change everything about his lifestyle.!
I on the other hand have made plans to leave the country.
Just finished school, its summertime, and there is a fire burning underneath my feet, I need to go, I sell my melodeon, my bicycle, and any other thing I can to raise the money, nobody want to see me leave.
I get no help from anyone:'
The day I leave, there no great good wishes for my onward journey, its all sadness, and self pity, to date my life has been surrounded by these sort of demonstrations.
But I grin a bear it, I need to get away, even though I have grown to love Uncle, the only father I have known,

he always showed me his love, shared his ideas, and all that he knew about life.
It is still not enough, there has to be more.
As the ship sails away I am looking back at Ireland, I am not sad, rather feeling excited about the great adventure I am about to begin.
Where it will take me I do not care.
I have very little money, in fact I have no plans at all, no place to stay when I get there, and nobody there to greet me, perhaps I'm crazy.
Looking down from the deck of the ship as she ploughs her way through the waves, I see white ripples of wash rolling over and over, looking ever so much like the furrows of earth used to do, when Uncle would plough the land.
Where did I come from I say to myself, how did I get here, I am a lost soul among a world of people, a world of people who all know each other, mothers, fathers, brothers, sisters, uncles, aunts, cousins:'
I have none, there is only me.
The thought of the future fills me with a feeling of an idea of success.
Maybe I will become a musician, maybe I will meet a nice girl, maybe I will fall in love, maybe I will have my own family, maybe I will find out who I really am, for now its just maybe, maybe.
Tonight I do not have a place to sleep, I have opted to stay indoors on the ship, I do not have any money for a

cabin, I fall asleep in one of the corridors.
Too soon awoken by the loud sound of the ships siren signalling its approach to port.
I rush outside to see the lights of the harbour, its very foggy and dark, with my small brown altar boy suitcase in hand, I see through windows of the ships restaurant people eating breakfast.
I feel hungry, but I don't have the money to buy any food, I must forget about hunger.
I think back to where I was reared, "so much food", even the dogs are well fed, and thinking about dogs, I would now eat theirs if I had it.
The ship pulls into port, and along with the rest of the passengers I disembark, then we all board a train, my final destination is London.
On the train ride to London, I walk through the restaurant carriage, people are leaving after their meal, more people are sitting down, I see remnants of uneaten bread on the little tables, feverously I grab them and stuff them into my pocket.
I am praying that no-one will see me, its only a few short steps to a toilet cubical, where I ravenously devour the crusts, followed by some tap water.
Looking out the windows of the train, we pass by many stations, place names I have never heard of, every now and then the ticket inspector passes by checking tickets, how soon will be before we get to London I ask him, not too long now he would say.

I never thought it could be so far away, I am stuck now, I feel trapped like the little animals rabbits, fox's, and hares we used to hunt and kill.
The bouncing sun is shining in through the carriage windows, people are putting on their coats, all of a sudden the ticket inspector make an announcement, next stop Paddington station.
It's the end of the line, Thank God I say.
The train slowly pulls in chuffing and puffing, smoke and steam billowing around the station .
I alight same as everyone else, not wishing to appear stupid I go with the flow.
I have never seen so many people so busy, I say to myself where are they all going, must be something important of course.
A man in a uniform is standing at the end by a gate, I ask him how I get to the centre of London, get the tube to Trafalgar Square he replies, a tube I say, "yes yes" its over there he points towards a tunnel.
I follow the crowd along with my brown altar boy suitcase in hand, down a very long staircase, we then reach a platform, wind is coming from somewhere I don't know.
Lights are now coming down the tunnel, I have never seen such a thing, then it pulls in and stops, it's a train I get on same as everyone, a lady sitting near the doorway smiles, I ask where is Trafalgar Square, next stop she says.

That was quick I am thinking, we all alight, again I follow the crowd up a long set of steps and out into the ever so bright sunlight, what a gorgeous day, a day fine enough for making hay.
But from here where do I go, I have not a clue, I walk with the sun on my right shoulder, the street I am on is so large, so much traffic, there are even a few horse's drawing beautiful green carriages.
Ah yes I see where they are going, it says Savoy Hotel, must be an important place in there.
I see a sign, it says Waterloo bridge, I gotta see this, my god what a huge river I say, I have never seen such a big river, sure our rivers at home are only like mikey mouse streams compared to this monster.
Either side of this bridge is a continual people march, and so much traffic, the air stinks with exhaust fumes.
With only two shillings in my pocket, I know I wont last long, but I must find somewhere to sleep tonight, maybe tomorrow will bring me some luck.
All I need a quite little spot, I know it wont be as easy as at home, where I could find a hayshed no problem, have a good nights sleep and be gone before sunrise.
There is nothing here except cold concrete, what will I do I cant face the thought of returning back to the farm, all of a sudden I get a brain wave.?
I see a pub as I walk back towards the way I came.
Its called the Lord Wellington.
Its right on a corner, maybe they might need a worker, I

walk in,
A woman is busy cleaning tables.
The place is busy, yeah she says wait there a while till I get the governor, I am thinking what is a governor, the only governor I know is the one to control the speed of a tractor.
A big tall man comes out from behind a counter, are you man looking for work, yes sir a answer.
Well he says I need a cellar man, can you do that, no problem I say, he laughs.
What experience have you, I tell him how much I know about farming, hunting, fishing, and I play music I tell him.
How old are you, you look very young, naw that's my appearance, I am 19 years old, "my god" you look as if you just out of primary school.
Anyway he said follow me, I walk behind him down a stair we go into the cellar below his pub,
Here downstairs in this almost dark room he shows me a big tank, its filled with beer bottles, look at these he says, I need a man to wash these, and to scrape all the labels off, when you have done that you will need to place them in bottle crates.
Can you do that sort of thing, no problem, he laughs again.
I'm not finished yet he says, its not as easy as that, not only do you wash and scrape, but you must fill them with Guinness from these casks, ah sure tis well I know about

Guinness and the casks I tell him, every year at home tis many the cask of Guinness I have helped out to the haggard to be drank.
I see where your coming from he replies.
When can you start .
Now I said.!
Great, now I will show you to your room, he brings me up four flights of stairs, into a small room, you will be sharing this with another boy:'
Come down stairs with me now, and have a bite to eat, I think he must be reading my mind:.
All the while as I am eating, trying not to appear so hungry, the chef who is almost finished for the day is asking, like a little bit more.
I really never had a big appetite, naw fine I say.
The governor walks by, is everything all right" brilliant, sir is it all right if I go for a walk.
Sure, tomorrow morning I will give you your rota, what the hell is a rota. I keep quite.
Go on he says, go down around the square, enjoy yourself. I am trilled, here I am at fifteen and a half, and I have it cracked open like an Easter egg on an Easter Sunday morning.
No one suspects my age.
Very happy I am as I stroll along, the busy street the rushing crowds all of a sudden I am part of it, its great. Wait till they hear about it at home.
Evening time approaches, I make my way back to the

pub, its busy,
I am introduced to the rest of the staff, and to his Lady wife, "a fine looking woman";
I sit in a corner of the pub until closing time, sipping lemonade and watching the people coming in and the people going out, the place is very smokey, I think back to Uncle and his pipe, there was such a lovely smell when he smoked his pipe.
I say hello to anyone who comes near me, I get no reply, they are not very friendly. I would never want to be like that.
Closing time comes, it's a big rush, drink up now I hear the governor shouting, the bar staff are busy picking up glasses, ashtrays, placing stools upside down on the seats that line the pub.
The marble tiled area at the edge of the bar is being mopped with a wet mop. With doors closed now that the last customer has gone, the staff begin to ready the bar for the morning trade.
Michael the boy I will be sharing the room with, gets friendly with me, come on he says we will go to the kitchen and have some tea.
In the kitchen he makes some sandwiches and a pot of tea, more staff come in, where's the tea, where's a my sandwiches, they jokily shout, shag off says Michael. Make your own.
Then its off up to our room, he is in the bed furthest away from the window, my bed is almost up against it.

We say goodnight to each other.!
Getting to sleep should be easy for me, its been a very long day, but my mind in a flurry of excitement, I have a bed, better than a hayshed.
I gaze out the windows at the flickering yellow neon lights, no stars tonight, a beautiful sky I cannot see.
Occasionally I catch a glimpse of the moon, the traffic is still moving, I wonder if they ever go to sleep.
Sometime later I drift off to sleep.
I wake up to the sound of a very loud bell, its an alarm clock going off.
Michael is cursing and swearing, bloody thing, t'would annoy St Peter he says.
He is up real fast, rushes to the bathroom, washes shaves, and dresses himself, I follow suit. Downstairs we go, breakfast is consumed fast, the governor comes on the scene, its your first day he tells me, you know of course you are only on trial, fine I say, I have no choice,.
I see the huge amount of bottles I have to wash:'
He gives me a pair of big rubber gloves, its all yours now me boy.
There are two very large tanks half filled with water, he explains that I have to put the bottles in one and allow to soak for a while, then I must remove and with a sharp scraper remove the labels.
When that is done, I place them into the second tank, this tank is filled with a cleansing fluid, not very nice smelling.

When they have been in that tank for over an hour I remove them to a crate, one by one.
This process is repeated over and over until all the bottles are cleaned and ready for bottling.
As evening comes the governor praises me, it's a good job you are doing, you will get on all right.
The job is yours.
A week has now passed by, I have not really missed the time slipping, the governor calls me, here is your pay packet he says, you'd want to do something about your cards, what cards I ask him, your tax and insurance he says, I'll tell you where to go, you will have to have them if you want to continue working here.
I go up to my room, it's a feeling of immense wonder my first wage, I count it over and over, its all of thirteen pounds ten shillings; I count it again.
I cant wait any longer, during the two hour break when the pub closes down from three a clock to five, I make my way to a music shop, and I spend most of it on a guitar, it cost most of my wage, not much left over, but I do have what I really want,
"A Guitar".
Back in my room later on I get a note pad, now I will write home, they still have not heard a word from me since I arrived here, all they know is that I have gone to London.
I could be anywhere.
My letter contains most of what has happened, with the

exception of dressing up my travels, I know that they will think very highly of me when they read of my great fortune.
No doubt the neighbours will hear of my escapades, already I am thinking of home, feeling homesick, yes I say, this place is really not for me, only for a while.
Describing my wage, " how much ", then my guitar, its colour, and my far flung intentions.
My letter is now finished and I need to post it, where is the post office I enquire, I am told its closed until Monday.
I get stamp from a staff member, put it in a post box they say, it will be picked up on Monday morning, with that now done I await in a state of glee.
Next week passes by more slowly or so it feels, nothing from home yet, the governor says to me did you give the phone number here, no I tell him, I was afraid.
I hope they got my letter,
I would love to hear what's happening back there.
How are the collie dogs.
My job is a five and a half day week, one and a half days off, the governor's wife calls me, I have a letter for you she says, I feel my heart my heart thumping in my chest with excitement.
I go up to my room, sit by the window on my bed:
Carefully opening the letter, I don't believe what I am reading,
It just can-not be, its impossible.

Ah no.!
" Uncle is dead".
He was buried almost a week ago the letter says.
I just cry cry and cry.
I realise now how much I love him.
The man who taught me so much:'
I will never see him again,
never hear his voice calling me.
" Mo Gile ".

Mo Gile Don't Be Shy

The pikes and spades are rusted
No horses grazing among the fields
Neither grain or roots produced
That farmhouse long since pulled down

Not a stone of that farmyard in place
Removed to make way for concrete
Where once was living community
Now is a dead forgotten memory

Today's people know little of its past
The glory days of sow and reap
Kinship and friendship
An argument here and there

A cup of tea a cold boiled spud
Respect for the Angelus Bell
Tip my hat as a lady walks by
Mo Gile dont be shy.

DRIMOLEAGUE RAILWAY STATION
WEST CORK, IRELAND.
1950's
After the fair was over, cattle were loaded onto the cattle carriages, and transported far and wide.

To each and everything in its own time
Respect.

The Ould Back Door

Den My Uncle by Oliver Keane
First published in 2009 by
Revilo production publications
Bishopstown, Cork City, Ireland.
www.oliverkane.com

Text © 2009 O.K.

Editing Design and Layout 2009-reviloproductions

Cover Picture
Is a Fairday in Dunmanway town
At the turn of the 20th century.!
Uncle Den is in the foreground.

Printed in Great Britain
by Amazon